INHERITING CHAOS WITH COMPASSION

INHERITING

CHAOS

WITH

COMPASSION

Learn to Navigate Your
Loved One's Financial Legacy

JENNIFER LUZZATTO

LIONCREST
PUBLISHING

INHERITING CHAOS WITH COMPASSION

Learn to Navigate Your Loved One's Financial Legacy

ISBN   978-1-5445-1313-3 *Paperback*
       978-1-5445-1312-6 *Ebook*

To my daughter Laura.

CONTENTS

INTRODUCTION

WHEN CHAOS HITS

In 2013, my husband was diagnosed with leukemia.

We both were overwhelmed and scared as he went through months of chemotherapy. The medical procedures, including a bone marrow transplant, were stressful for both of us. We set up our finances to manage his care, and we prepared for the worst.

Then, miraculously, the bone marrow transplant worked.

We thought he was cured.

Our life resumed a sense of normalcy. He went back to work. With his compromised immune system, our new normal was slightly different, but we made plans, bought a house, and began renovations, preparing with our nine-year-old daughter to move in. We planned a family trip to Alaska.

Then, almost two years to the day from his original diagnosis, we found out my husband's cancer was back with a vengeance. He began treatment right away.

Six weeks later, I tried to call him from work, but he didn't answer the phone. I grabbed a sandwich to bring him for lunch. When I got home, he was in bed. "I just need to sleep," he said.

As the night wore on, he started breathing funny. I called his doctors, but even after I did what they told me, he got worse—and still worse. At ten o'clock, I called 911. Paramedics arrived, but he refused to go with them. I couldn't get him out of bed. The medics informed me that if someone is awake and unwilling, they can't make them go to the hospital.

At two in the morning, I called 911 again. Again, he refused to go in the ambulance. He only wanted to sleep. "That's fine," I said, "but we're getting up at six. I'm calling 911, and they're going to put you in the car. I'm taking you down there."

That morning, the medics didn't leave, even though he

still refused their help. I think they knew he was dying, even though I didn't. Finally, he needed to go to the bathroom, and while he was up, I convinced him to get in a chair so they could carry him down the stairs.

They whisked him off to the emergency room, where doctors intubated and stabilized him in the critical care unit.

His heart stopped.

The hospital staff resuscitated him.

"How many times do you want us to do that before we don't do it anymore?" someone asked me. They were trying not to freak me out, but I didn't understand what was happening.

"I don't know," I said.

While I sat with him, his heart stopped again, and they resuscitated him a second time. A nurse pulled me aside.

"Do you really want us to do this?" she asked. "He's not going to get better."

I didn't have time to think about it. "No," I said. "Don't make him suffer any more."

Once you make the decision to stop care, it's done. He died right there in front of me. His body just couldn't take it anymore. I went home to tell my nine-year-old daughter.

* * *

Our experience was a shock, but it was not unique. All of us face loss, and some of us face loss unexpectedly and early in life. After a trauma like the one my daughter and I endured, those who remain face essential tasks that are not really that hard but which create time-consuming pain.

Everything was disrupted. My family had been in the middle of moving to a new house. There was the planned family trip to Alaska, which we ended up joining, and though I was in shock the whole time, it was good for my daughter to get out of Dodge. I had a closet full of my husband's clothes that I would never need and so much paperwork to complete. I had to get the death certificate and deal with the health insurance, life insurance, and stocks he had acquired through his employer.

As a financial planner, I knew all the pieces that someone must deal with in my situation. I knew how to handle my husband's accounts, and I was familiar with the many forms. Yet, I panicked over health insurance and home renovations and his income having gone away. Some days,

I couldn't wait to get to dinner and have a glass of wine. For the next year, I was kind of numb, going through the motions, fulfilling obligations, and trying to keep myself from exhaustion.

It was a long process to take care of things and create a new routine. After trauma, we never really go back, but we establish how we're going to live again. My daughter and I became the "girl team." We leaned into a robust life of connecting with her friends and their moms and my girlfriends. The dynamic of our home and our finances changed, and we constructed a new normal.

In December 2017, my sister died suddenly and unexpectedly. Her death pitched me back into chaos as I managed her estate and her husband's care. That's a story for a little later. But now, when I sit in my office with clients who have lost someone, and they describe their story and their pain, they usually end with, "It's all so overwhelming, you know?"

Yes. I know.

BEGIN WHERE YOU ARE

The death of a loved one creates chaos in our lives. There are so many decisions to be made, and our fear of making the wrong choices can be paralyzing. We find ourselves asking, *What's the next step? How will I do it? Will I do it right?* When we're drowning in big emotions, managing the financial aftermath becomes a part-time job we don't want.

If you are in this situation, you may feel there is a big mess in front of you right now. It can be organized. Even in chaos, you can figure out where you are financially and where you can go from there. You can put the pieces together, organize the confusion, and create a financial plan that's easily managed.

On the other side of this chaos, there's so much freedom.

This book will show you how to take measured and meaningful steps to organize the finances in front of you, whether they're yours or an estate you've been left to manage. It's imperative that you break everything down into doable and bite-sized pieces. In this book, I'll show you the basics of how to begin, and you'll gain confidence to work with a financial advisor you trust. A great relationship with a financial advisor can take so much of the logistical burden off your plate, so you can focus on your new normal.

UNDERSTANDING FINANCES THROUGH RELATIONSHIPS

The death of my husband, and then my sister—very major life experiences—taught me how to organize the work of dealing with a loved one's estate, while having compassion for my own emotional journey. Neither death was expected. I was organized and knowledgeable about the financial picture before my husband's death and completely blindsided by my sister's. I understand how our emotional burdens impact our financial lives.

When clients come to us, we ask them everything. Sometimes that "everything" has nothing to do with number crunching, but it gives us a trail of clues that helps us pull together a complete picture of our clients' lives. Some advisors are more transactional and feel they don't necessarily need the whole picture to sell financial products, but I was never interested in being that kind of advisor.

I started my career as a trader and administrative support in the bond room at a regional brokerage firm. In this commission based environment, I was in the background doing the grunt work and learning to trade securities. During that time, I started to realize the value of relationships to guide these transactions. Unless you know someone's situation, it's harder to determine how they should invest their money. You need to know what you're investing towards.

I changed jobs and worked at a bank, where my boss was a Certified Financial Planner (CFP). As I transitioned to become a portfolio manager, I began studying for my Chartered Financial Analyst (CFA) designation, and I was in school for my MBA. The pieces fell into place, and I realized that fee-only advisors like my boss could give advice and build relationships to serve their clients. The beauty of the world of fee-only advisors is that, because they aren't chasing commissions, they are happy to share their knowledge and experience with other advisors. It was a relief to think I could take my experience and education and apply it to a business model I would love. I went for my CFP designation and started Summit Financial Partners, a fee-only financial planning firm.

It is a gift to connect with my clients, listen to what they're going through, and understand how that impacts their financial lives. I have a unique connection with clients who have inherited chaos after a loved one's passing. I know firsthand that they can get through what they're facing. With patience and compassion, we can conquer the chaos.

ONE STEP AT A TIME

Part one of this book addresses the financial legacy your loved one has left behind. You'll learn the different roles and responsibilities of settling an estate and how to get organized and tackle these new responsibilities in small pieces. You'll gain a high-level understanding of how to work with professionals who can advise you through the process and take much of the financial load off your plate.

In part two, you'll find a primer for understanding and incorporating inheritance into your own finances. You'll learn the basics of the accounts and investments you may encounter in your loved one's estate, and you'll understand how to pivot these investments into a plan that works for you. Finally, we'll discuss some of the basics of setting up your own legacy to pass on to others.

What you won't find here is a step-by-step guide for how to set up your own financial plan. Everyone's situation is unique, and your specific circumstances should be considered and built into the best plan for you. You will understand financial language in clear terms, so you can ask clarifying questions and communicate your needs for your financial future with a financial advisor, if you decide to work with one.

Taking on a loved one's financial legacy can be an overwhelming responsibility. Together, we will find the pieces of this financial puzzle, and we'll connect them one at a time. My story is not unique by any stretch of the imagination. At some point in our lives, we all deal with the chaos of losing a loved one. With time and patience, in small steps, the financial chaos can be organized into a new financial picture that supports your life and how you want to live it.

PART ONE

FROM PAST TO PRESENT: HOW TO MANAGE FINANCIAL CHAOS

Chapter One

DEFINING ROLES

The most challenging aspect of managing a deceased loved one's estate is the paralysis of not knowing what to do next. *What is my next step? How do I do it? When do I do it? Will I do it right?* It's imperative to break everything down into doable, bite-sized pieces.

When my sister died, no thought had been given to how someone might pick up the pieces. Mary wasn't organized in her finances, and her husband Stan was in cognitive decline. She died suddenly at home, likely from a heart attack. Stan didn't call 911. He called my parents and told them that Mary, who had a small craft business, "can't paint anymore." My mom probed with questions: *Is Mary sick?* No. *Did she have an accident?* No. *Did she have an asthma attack, or a seizure?*

Finally, she asked, "Stan, did Mary die?"

"Yes," he replied.

Stan was named the executor of Mary's estate, meaning he was responsible for resolving her assets. We'll define that role in more depth shortly. But Stan needed help— not just to manage the finances but to arrange his ongoing medical care.

We visited an attorney to have Stan sign a document declining to serve as executor. I left the attorney's office with two roles: executor of my sister's estate and power of attorney for her husband.

Taking on this responsibility meant taking on a big unknown. When my husband Eric died, I was struck with the heavy emotional blow, but I already had full knowledge of our finances and the logistical steps that I needed to take. Taking on my sister's estate was complete chaos. I didn't know their bills, their investments, or their needs, and I was immediately thrown into the tasks of cleaning out their house, setting Stan up in assisted living, selling their home and cars, and coming to terms with the long-term financial plans Stan would need to support his future.

These documents that declared me as executor and power

of attorney gave me authority, but no one told me what to do. At times, these responsibilities felt overwhelming, and it was tough to know where to start. There were so many threads in Mary's finances and Stan's care to follow and tie off. Through understanding my responsibilities in the role of executor and power of attorney, my first steps began to take shape.

UNDERSTANDING RESPONSIBILITIES

We'll discuss how to begin organizing finances in the next chapter, but first we'll define the roles and responsibilities for each person managing a loved one's estate. To begin, it's important to define three terms: power of attorney, executor, and beneficiary.

POWER OF ATTORNEY

Power of attorney is given to a person who has the legal authority to act on someone else's behalf while that person (called the "principal") is still alive. This role primarily refers to financial decisions, but as you'll see, power of attorney can be established for medical decision-making as well. In some cases, power of attorney is granted if someone is declared incapacitated through legal and medical means.

A person with power of attorney over someone's financial

matters can open and close accounts, write checks, sell assets, plan the estate, and otherwise operate in place of that person for all financial matters. There are a few types of power of attorney worth noting: durable, nondurable, medical, and springing.

Durable Power of Attorney

A durable power of attorney is effective immediately, and it only expires on the principal's death. In two separate examples, I have my mother named as my durable power of attorney, and I am the power of attorney for my sister's husband, Stan. In the case of my mother, I named her my power of attorney so that, if something were to happen to me, she wouldn't have to go to court to establish the authority to make decisions on my behalf. There is no triggering event to put a durable power of attorney in effect.

In Stan's case, he is incapacitated, and my role as power of attorney allows me to settle my sister's estate and set up Stan's care for as long as he needs because there is no time limit to this type of power of attorney.

Nondurable Power of Attorney

Nondurable power of attorney is for a set period of time. This structure can be used to give someone legal decision-making power in place of the principal for a single transaction, and it can be set to expire after the event is over. This power of attorney is especially useful if one has a spouse who travels a lot. For example, if a couple are buying a house, nondurable power of attorney would allow one spouse to sign for the other, but it could be set to end after that transaction.

Medical Power of Attorney

A medical power of attorney is set up to grant another person the power to make healthcare decisions for the principal, particularly when they are incapacitated.

Springing Power of Attorney

This structure "springs into action" at a future date when a specific event occurs. Springing power of attorney can be set up to give someone authority after the principal has had an accident, becomes incapacitated, or had another triggering event that has been decided in advance.

Choosing the Right Person for Power of Attorney

When deciding who should hold power of attorney, it's incredibly important to choose someone you trust. Once it's made active, this person has the authority to make legal, financial, or medical decisions for you.

As I mentioned above, my mother has my power of attorney. I have a twelve-year-old daughter, and it's important to me to have structures in place for my mother to make decisions for my daughter and my estate if needed. My mother can even write a check out in my name if she has the right paperwork to prove it. I completely trust my mother and having the power of attorney in effect makes it easier for her to immediately care for my daughter if anything were to happen to me.

EXECUTOR

The role of the executor is to make sure an estate is divided and distributed properly in accordance with how the will states things should be. When someone leaves money to a person or organization in their will, the executor is responsible for making sure that money is distributed to the appropriate parties. The executor drives the process of proving the will (known as "probate") and distributing assets.

In the first step, the executor takes the will to a court to prove that it is the valid last testament of the deceased. Not all wills go through probate. In some cases, an estate has too few assets for probate to be necessary. Some assets can be passed directly to the beneficiary without going through an executor. When a spouse dies, jointly-owned property passes directly to the surviving spouse with no need to consult the will or involve the executor. One example of this is a home that two spouses own as joint tenants with rights of survivorship: when one spouse dies, the surviving spouse becomes the sole owner. Another structure that can be set up to bypass a will is a trust. Trust funds can hold assets and dictate how they are distributed, so a will and an executor are not needed to transfer these funds to the beneficiary. You'll learn more about trusts and how they work in chapter 7 on estate planning.

If you are stepping into the executor role, an estate attorney can be helpful in determining whether a will needs to go through probate and how the wishes of the will should be carried out.

Once the will is verified, the executor is responsible for making sure that assets are distributed according to the will. The executor contacts companies (such as investment or retirement accounts) that hold assets to let them know a triggering event has happened and they are to transfer assets to the appropriate beneficiary (we'll get to exactly what a beneficiary is next).

The executor is accountable to the county or municipality where the deceased person lived, and they report how the assets were distributed to the commissioner of accounts. Counties vary in how exacting the records must be on an estate. For example, the county where my sister lived wanted to know to the penny that I'd done what I was supposed to do with her assets. My record keeping had to be very exacting and detailed.

Executors can draw a fee for the work of distributing the estate, and they must show that the fees they're taking are reasonable. Family members and survivors are not the only people who can serve as executors; an attorney can be hired for this role. A paid executor can be beneficial if there's a lack of trust between siblings or if the task seems too large for the person that was named the executor.

The executor is also responsible for settling the costs of the funeral. Life insurance policies are often used to cover those expenses, or the cost may come out of that person's assets. A word of compassion here: when the executor is a family member, they often feel a lot of guilt around making the best decisions and purchases around the funeral. It doesn't add value to buy the most expensive casket and vault and grave marker, or to take on guilt over those decisions. Over time, the impact of those details fades away.

Being an executor is a part-time job. If you've already begun to step into this role, you know the nature of the burden. It is frustrating, exhausting, and tiring work. You have to understand the paperwork required at each step. You'll spend time going to the bank, calling insurance companies, and transferring investment accounts. You might spend several days sitting and waiting at the Department of Motor Vehicles. You'll spend an inordinate amount of time on the phone. You may want to burn down the buildings of companies that make your paperwork and your job harder. Operating in the financial world, I already understood how to do most of the job of executor, and yet my sister's relatively simple estate took four solid weeks of work time over six months.

It is possible to lighten the load, one small piece at a time. The first task is to learn where all the pieces of the financial puzzle are so you can begin to organize them and make a plan to deal with each account. In the next chapter, we'll discuss how to find all the accounts, bills, and plans that need to be dealt with, and then we'll lay out a hierarchy for when—and how—to resolve each piece.

You don't have to do this job alone. Part of the process of being an executor is recognizing how many responsibilities you can tackle effectively and how many might be necessary to hire out. An attorney or paralegal can help you understand your responsibilities and reporting requirements. As we'll see in the next chapter, a financial planner can help uncover and sort the various accounts that are to be distributed.

As an executor, you'll need to keep clear records. It's beneficial to be organized and detail-oriented, so that you can take one small step at a time toward resolving the estate.

BENEFICIARY

In financial terms, the word "beneficiary" is used to describe recipients of assets from a will, trust, retirement account, or insurance policy. Upon a person's death, the beneficiaries named on their accounts become the automatic owners of those assets. The transfer of those assets skips the estate process and goes directly to the beneficiary. Typically, the beneficiary would need to open an account with the brokerage firm that owns the asset, and from there, the brokerage firm would transfer the inherited funds to the beneficiary's new account.

Being a beneficiary comes with a few responsibilities. They usually have to open an account in their name as the inheritor to receive their assets. The executor will usually drive the process of getting assets moved by reporting the triggering event. For example, if there is a Vanguard account that is to be transferred to a beneficiary, the executor would present the death certificate and Vanguard would contact the beneficiary to get the ball rolling. The beneficiary would then have to call or come in to open the appropriate accounts. A beneficiary can also go directly to

Vanguard and present the death certificate to get started, but this responsibility usually falls on the executor.

Beneficiary designations trump any contradicting plans stated in the will. This means that if a retirement account has one beneficiary listed, but the will states the retirement money should go to a different person, the beneficiary designation on the account will be honored over the wishes in the will.

In a notable example, there was a case of a woman in New York City who set up her retirement accounts when she was fresh out of college and named her sister as her beneficiary. She later married, but never revisited her beneficiary designation. After fifty years of marriage, she passed away. All of the money that she intended to go to her husband went to her sister instead. The beneficiary designation trumped the will, and legally, the money became her sister's, even though it wasn't the woman's intention. This decision was upheld in court, and the husband was out of luck.

I ask my clients to review their accounts once a year to make sure the beneficiary designations are current and correct. It's incredibly important to keep these designations current, and they take only a few minutes to update.

ONE STEP AT A TIME

Before you can begin looking into a loved one's accounts and assets, you'll need to have the legal authority established to ask questions and gather information. An attorney can guide you to have the documentation in place if you're serving as an executor or have power of attorney. With clear guidelines for the responsibilities of each role in the process, you can begin the first steps to organize and resolve the pieces of a loved one's estate. You'll learn how to begin gathering accounts and sorting documentation in the next chapter. We'll take this one small step at a time.

Chapter Two

———

GETTING ORGANIZED

I began managing my sister's estate and my brother-in-law's care in the same way I manage many things in life: with a to-do list. Understanding their financial life was a matter of following pieces and clues, and my list grew longer with each one. With six bank accounts at three different banks, missing car titles, and investment accounts with no statements, it was overwhelming to see more items pile on to the list faster than I could check them off.

I would file a form only to figure out that three more forms were required. I would do one tiny step and then wait to see what new steps were needed. It felt like tasks just came out of the woodwork at me. There was no quick fix; every accomplishment was one step forward and a half step back.

Yet, in tiny increments, I made progress one step at a time. At one point, I was dedicating one afternoon a week to getting through different pieces of my sister's will. I'd strategically plan an afternoon at the DMV for a Wednesday at 3 p.m. when it was least busy. Blocking out time this way helped alleviate the feeling of being overwhelmed. If I didn't get my one piece resolved at the DMV that day, I went back the next day. I made lists of the steps that needed to be done with each institution, so that I could methodically work my way through them.

It is possible to lighten the load, one small piece at a time. The first task is to learn where all the pieces of the financial puzzle are, so you can begin to organize them and make a plan to deal with each account.

BRING EVERYTHING OUT OF THE WOODWORK

Everybody has piles of mail and papers somewhere, and these are the best first clues when looking for a loved one's accounts. You can find a lot of important account information in those piles. It can be an unpleasant task to sort through these papers, but it's a necessary one. In the case of my sister, my mother actually found the will in a pile of papers. It wasn't filed anywhere. We also found some things too late: my sister had some desires for her funeral that we didn't know about until we found her specifications after the fact.

Even when you're organized and proactive, you may find yourself putting out fires. Recently, I was surprised by a phone call about Stan's prescriptions. Whoever set up his prescriptions at his assisted living facility had written down the wrong name and address for me. Several months later, I received a phone call: apparently, Stan's medications had not been paid since January. It was July. The bill was $5,000. I never received the bills for his medication. The company was about to cut off his medication. We were able to pay the bill just in time.

Sometimes you have to wait for details like this to come to you. The more organized you can make the accounts you do know about, the easier it will be to deal with surprises.

When embarking on this journey, the biggest clues are in the mail. Whether it's an electricity bill or a retirement account, most companies will send notices on a monthly or quarterly basis. Each of these notices can give you details about the account number and who to contact.

FORWARDING MAIL

As executor and power of attorney, I went to the post office and had all my sister's mail forwarded to me. Although this might seem like a lot, it's always better to start out with more information about someone's finances and then wean it down if it's not relevant.

You can easily have mail forwarded by visiting a post office and giving them your forwarding address. You'll need documentation that names you as executor or power of attorney for your loved one to set this up.

Keep an eye on the mail for one year. This is the maximum mail cycle for accounts that send yearly statements, so you can be confident that you've received notices from all the companies that hold assets or debts.

CHECKING BANK STATEMENTS

You can comb through bank statements to see if any random deposits were made into an account. For example, you may not have a statement for a retirement account— and therefore you don't know it exists—but you may see a withdrawal you don't recognize leaving a bank account. This withdrawal would have information attached to it that you could track down and then use to see where the money was deposited.

FINDING ELECTRONIC STATEMENTS

Although mail is one of the best ways to start piecing things together, this isn't a foolproof solution. If your loved one received statements electronically, their account information may be in an email account that you don't have access to.

Look for email logins, so you can check your loved one's inbox. Bills could become overdue or insurance could go unpaid, and you may not know until you get a phone call.

If possible, it's best to have a list of all accounts and passwords ahead of time. In order to be proactive, I recommend people print and file one statement annually. Even this small amount of information is so much better than going in cold with nobody to ask.

SEARCHING THE STATE DATABASE FOR UNCLAIMED ASSETS

Another potential avenue to find assets is the state's database for unclaimed assets. When property or assets go unclaimed, they are turned over to the state. Each company that holds an asset will first attempt to contact the beneficiary before reporting it as unclaimed, so it can take years for these assets to show up at the state department. Through each state's Department of the Treasury website, you can find a Division of Unclaimed Property.

It's a good idea to search in each state the deceased lived in, and to check back each year.

I also recommend searching your own name, both in your state's database and at the institutions that hold your loved one's assets, just in case you may have inherited something without knowing.

HIDDEN TREASURE

You may find clues that need further investigation. Be careful not to throw out items that could be useful. Not everything you find will be a "good asset" that holds a lot of wealth, but it's always worth looking into.

Different generations hold differing ideas on how to handle money, and this influences how people invest and where they put their assets. For example, people who went through the Great Depression tend to be less trustful of banks and financial institutions. Occasionally my clients have found assets hidden in their parents' houses: keys to lock boxes, paper bills stuffed in the pages of books—and I've even heard one story of a woman finding diamonds hidden in a rolled-up newspaper. It's important to check everything before tossing items or papers.

WHAT TO THROW OUT

As you organize papers and decide what to throw away, you want to look out for anything that has a dollar amount attached to it. Whether they're bills or financial accounts, these documents are your clues for what debts and assets the estate has.

However, there's no need to keep old statements and bills as long as you have the most recent statement to reference. It's recommended to keep the most recent seven years of tax returns, but it's not necessary to hold on to the last twenty years of tax paperwork in the attic.

You'll use these statements to identify what institutions to look into, and where your trails begin. Once you're in contact with the institutions that are connected with your loved one's estate, you'll be able to access all the necessary account history. You can let the older paperwork go.

IDENTIFYING TOP PRIORITIES

The first documents to address are bills for insurance or utilities that the survivors might still need. This includes medical, life, property, and casualty insurance, as well as electricity, water, and gas bills. You don't want power to get cut off in mid-January's freezing cold if an elderly person is living in their own home. Losing medical insurance can be a nightmare for survivors. It's important to have property and casualty insurance to protect assets in the case of an accident or natural disaster, so that the survivor isn't at risk of losing their home. Property and casualty insurance can sometimes be reinstated if the policy lapses, but health and life insurance policies can't be put back in place once you stop paying the premiums. It's important to know whether they're needed before you let them go.

INHERITING DEBT

When a loved one dies, their personal consumer debts, such as credit cards, are paid with assets from the estate. For this reason, the county's commissioner of accounts may require the executor to wait one year to fully close out the estate, so that if a debt surfaces, the money is still there to pay it. If there's not enough money in the estate to cover a debt, the debt is typically dismissed.

Jointly-owned debt, such as a credit card in both spouse's names, transfers to the surviving owner. Joint debt can go unnoticed when, for example, a spouse doesn't pay attention to the couple's finances, and discovering debts like this can come as a shock.

A friend of mine experienced this. Her father had cancer when she was very little, and in the years before he died, he racked up considerable credit card debt on an account that was also in her mother's name. When he died, my friend's mother was pitched into chaos: previously a stay-at-home mom with four kids, she had to get a job to work off the crushing debt. It took several years to get rid of it, and the saving grace was a small family beach property that she was able to sell to cover the last of it.

Because of her lack of knowledge of her finances, she had no idea this debt was coming her way. She trusted her husband, and she was overwhelmed with the stress of caring for her sick spouse and her four children. My friend decided that in her own partnership, she would never not know her finances. She is now married, owns a business with her husband, and has full knowledge of her financial situation.

The aftermath of a loved one's death can lead to debt as well. A death in a partnership can mean a loss of income for the survivor. A client of mine had a job she loved, but she wasn't highly paid, and when her husband died, her expenses were greater than her income. She maxed out all of the debt she had access to, until she was paying a quarter of her income on interest alone. She was hobbled by it. We found an unconventional solution for her: she had paid off her mortgage with her husband's insurance money, so she got a home equity loan to pay off her debt and reduce her interest. She will continue to work on this debt for years to come, but we were able to make it much less painful and penalizing.

In cases like these, it's important to chip away at the debt a little bit at a time. When clients have multiple debts, I encourage them to pay a little bit extra on their smallest debt to pay it off as quickly as they can. Once the smallest debt is paid off, they can take the amount they were paying to that account and add it to their payment for the next smallest debt. In this way, the payments create a snowball effect that cleans up debts along the way, from smallest to largest.

TACKLING ONE INSTITUTION AT A TIME

Once you have gathered all the papers you can find, begin to group them by institution. You may not yet know what each account is, or what's important, but organizing like papers together will give you a picture of all the institutions involved. A financial advisor can review these documents with you and guide you through the process of calling each institution to see what accounts your loved one held there, and what steps need to be taken to transfer those assets.

Once you have the paperwork grouped by institution, create a list of all the institutions you need to call. You can tackle all the accounts at that institution on the same phone call. In my experience, working with one institution at a time gives order to the chaos.

When you make these phone calls, you'll first need to

establish your authority to take action with accounts at each institution. You'll need to provide a copy of your affidavit of executor or power of attorney, as well as identifying information for the account holder: their Social Security number, birthdate, and address.

Next, you'll ask about the account that you know is with the institution. Each institution can search the Social Security number for any other accounts in your loved one's name, so ask if any other accounts exist for them.

Finally, you'll ask what paperwork the institution requires to move the assets into another person's name. They may require additional proof, such as a copy of the death certificate, and typically these documents will need a notarized signature. More steps may be added to get paperwork notarized before it can be submitted.

Usually, the beneficiary will need to open a new account and transfer the inherited funds into it. In some cases, the beneficiary will want their accounts created with a different bank or brokerage firm, and it's a multistep process to transfer funds from one institution to another.

Of course, it's never easy to get through all the bureaucracy and processing time it takes to approve paperwork. Breaking down all items on your list into bite-sized tasks will help make a larger task seem more manageable. Imposing an arbitrary end date for completing all tasks can be tempting, but in my experience, it only adds unnecessarily to the stress. You will run into roadblocks, and it will be less painful to do so if you work bit by bit.

Once all the accounts have been identified, transferred to the appropriate beneficiaries, and reported to the commissioner of accounts, the job of the executor is done. For the beneficiaries, the next step is to organize and consolidate the assets they're inheriting.

SIMPLIFYING ASSETS

With the transfers completed, the next step for the heir to simplify their newly inherited accounts is to gather the funds into one account to make investments and disbursements. Here's where a financial advisor can become invaluable, by taking all the confusion of transferring and investing money and making some sense of it. A financial advisor can tell you what paperwork is needed, fill it out for you, describe what it means, tell you where to sign, and take care of all the necessary steps. They can lighten the load.

Inherited finances become easier to manage when they're gathered into as few accounts as possible. Accounts of the same type can be consolidated; for example, separate IRA accounts can be combined into one. However, you can't mix different account types, such as an IRA with a taxable account. The key is to minimize the number of accounts you're managing.

The process to collecting assets into one place can be complex, and it varies depending on the institution holding the asset. A new account must be opened in the heir's name at the same institution where the deceased person's account is already held. The executor then signs a letter of instruction to the institution, letting them know the new account is open and how the assets are to be distributed. Once the new account is funded, investments can be made. If you're transferring these assets on your own, you'll need to learn the steps required by the institution you're working with and decide how you wish to invest the inheritance.

If you work with a financial advisor, they'll walk you through all these steps from the beginning and pull all these assets into one place with one custodian, such as TD Ameritrade. It's also possible to manage your own investment action through a brokerage platform like E-Trade. We'll discuss how to identify your goals and plan new investments in part two.

The key to conquering this complicated and multistepped approach is to simplify as much as possible, as early as possible. No matter what, the process is going to require a lot of patience to get it done properly. One step at a time, you will get closer to resolution.

Resolving my sister's estate taught me the importance of having financial information organized and accessible. When you don't have a close family member who has good knowledge of the financial picture, organization becomes even more important. When a loved one dies, many pieces of their financial picture can be hard to find. Professionals—from financial advisors to accountants to attorneys—can help you see the clues more clearly, as you'll see in the next chapter.

Chapter Three

———

LEANING ON PROFESSIONALS

The year after my sister died, I hit another roadblock I didn't see coming. Mary ran a craft business out of her home and I needed to file her taxes, but I couldn't find any records of what she'd sold or spent on supplies in the past year. I was completely in the dark about what to report to the government. Luckily, I found her prior year's tax return. It was my first clue to begin the process.

It turns out her husband had been the one keeping careful track of her business's financial records over the years, but in that last year, his memory had been failing him. He couldn't recall any of the information I needed.

I have relationships with certified public accountants

(CPAs), so I called one of them and explained the situation. He explained that the best thing we could do was explain our situation to the IRS and file estimated taxes based on the previous year's figures. The tax return was simple enough, but I wasn't qualified to defend myself in front of the IRS. By helping me prepare the tax return, the CPA was signing on to help defend the filing if the IRS had questions. I was in a vulnerable position, but I felt confident with a CPA helping me with this responsibility.

Developing relationships with professionals can seem expensive on the surface, but when you really need assistance, these are invaluable relationships to lean on. As you organize your loved one's papers, look for any professionals they worked with. These professionals will have records of their past business together, and in a case like my sister's tax return, they can more easily make assumptions around your loved one's business. These relationships save you time and energy searching for records, filing forms, and making decisions.

The emotional burden of losing a loved one is heavy enough. As you navigate their estate, it's invaluable to have professionals assist with the work of organizing finances. In this chapter, we'll discuss what financial advisors, accountants, and estate planning attorneys can do to lighten the load.

FINANCIAL ADVISORS

Financial advisors, also known as investment advisors, are at the epicenter of organizing the financial landscape, both in the wake of a death and at the start of planning your future. Advisors can assist you in finding all the pieces that are coming in. They can organize the estate's assets, create plans for debt, and coordinate new accounts.

Advisors ask—and find the answers for—all the questions that an executor deals with. *Are there bills to be taken care of? Who are the heirs, and what assets will they receive? Do we need a CPA to assist with taxes?* An advisor can clarify these questions and serve as the point of organization.

In settling an estate, the hardest part for the uninitiated—executors and beneficiaries alike—is the paperwork. The documentation required to open accounts, transfer funds, and manage investments is written in the language of the financial industry, and it can be difficult to understand for those who don't read it every day. Financial advisors understand this language, and they can help an executor sort out the transfers required to settle the estate as well as the records that need to be filed once those transfers are complete.

A financial advisor can help the beneficiary navigate the transfer of funds into the beneficiary's name, and the advisor can help choose the investments that fit the beneficiary's needs.

For an executor looking for support with settling an estate, it's best to work with a financial advisor that the beneficiary has already enlisted or one with whom they are comfortable working. The beneficiaries are the ones who will ultimately manage the accounts being transferred to them, so it can streamline the process for their advisors to be the primary points of contact. This means that an executor could be collaborating with a few advisors, if each beneficiary has a separate financial advisor. For example, if several siblings are inheriting their mother's estate, and each family member has their own advisor, the executor could connect with each of those advisors for help in getting the proper funds transferred to each sibling. The executor would need the agreement of each of the siblings to work with their advisors, but bringing these professionals on board could drastically simplify the paperwork and steps involved in settling the estate.

There are varying degrees of financial planning offered by advisors, and it's important to ask if an advisor's services meet your needs. Some advisors offer basic overviews of a client situation and make recommendations from there. Some advisors are keen to sell financial products and investments. The most comprehensive advisors will pull every pertinent piece of financial information together and create a plan to see what sort of life that financial picture will support for you. They'll advise how much you can spend, how much you should be saving, and what investment portfolios match your goals.

The financial advisor is the professional on your team who can dig deeper into assets, understand what they are and how they function, and give guidance on how they can be invested.

FEE-ONLY ADVISORS

The fee structures that advisors use vary, and they can be difficult to understand. There are two basic types of advisors: commission-based advisors and fee-only advisors. In the first model, advisors are paid through commissions when they sell investments and financial products. This means that the client doesn't pay the advisor directly; the advisor receives commissions from the institutions whose investments and packages they sell.

A second way advisors can be paid is through a percentage of the invested assets in the form of an "assets under management" fee (AUM). Advisors who do not take commissions are referred to as fee-only advisors. They are paid through AUM fees, hourly rates, and yearly retainers. Because they aren't swayed by commissions, they are free to advise with the client's best interest in mind.

Finally, advisors can charge an hourly rate, which they may institute for extra work, such as assisting an executor with paperwork on accounts the advisor doesn't manage themselves. There is no national average for these rates, but they can fluctuate between $150–300 per hour based on the complexity of the situation.

Advisors can mix these fees but not on the same asset. For example, if they have earned a commission from selling a particular investment to a client, they cannot also take an AUM fee on the same investment.

A great resource to find a fee-only advisor is the website for the National Association of Personal Financial Advisors (www.napfa.org). NAPFA is an organization of fee-only advisors, and their website gives more information about fee-only structures, as well as a database to find a fee-only advisor near you.

In addition to looking for a fee-only advisor, you can vet potential advisors by checking out their credentials. Advisors who have a Certified Financial Planner (CFP) or Chartered Financial Analyst (CFA) designation have passed stringent certifications.

It's worth taking the time to find an advisor with whom you can develop a good relationship. If you don't gel with an advisor, you're less likely to believe or follow through with their advice. You may need to talk to a few advisors before you find one whose fee structure you understand and feel comfortable with.

CERTIFIED PUBLIC ACCOUNTANTS

A step up from standard accountants, CPAs pass an exam to demonstrate their knowledge base, and this certification gives them expert standing with the IRS. When you work with a CPA, you have assurance that they have taken their education to a higher level. CPAs and accountants assist in preparing tax returns, and they can research technical terms and codes that would be mind-numbing to the average person. Taxes aren't as black and white as they seem, and a CPA can sort through the complexity to find the best solutions for you.

As your tax preparer, CPAs also sign your tax return with you, making them responsible in the case of an audit.

Many CPAs don't provide tax planning services, but financial advisors do, and an advisor will often consult with a CPA to make sure their strategies are sound from a tax perspective.

ESTATE PLANNING ATTORNEYS

The primary function of an estate planning attorney, as

the name suggests, is to plan the legal directives of an estate before death. After a death, an estate planning attorney can be a useful partner for an executor. They help you understand whether a will needs to go through probate, how assets are required to be distributed to heirs, and what reporting requirements you may have to give to the county's commissioner of accounts. Estate planning attorneys can also be hired to serve as executors.

In the case of my sister's death, my brother-in-law was her appointed executor, and he wasn't capable of serving this role. We visited an estate planning attorney to draft documents for Stan to recuse himself from serving as executor, and to assign me in his place. I also worked with an estate planning attorney to help me report to the commissioner of accounts on my sister's estate.

Additionally, estate planning attorneys can help you resolve any issues that arise from a will. My husband and I used an off-the-shelf software product to draft our will, but it didn't address certain legal issues properly, and I had to go to an estate planning attorney after he died to resolve questions in how we'd planned our estate.

Some of these duties aren't difficult, but it's crucial to do them right, and an estate planning attorney can guide you through those steps.

Lastly, estate planning attorneys can draft wills and trusts for your own assets. We'll discuss estate planning in depth in chapter 7.

COLLABORATING EFFECTIVELY

Settling an estate becomes much easier when you can pull all three of these roles together. In settling my sister's estate, I talked to and leaned on each of these professionals along the way. To collaborate effectively, you'll need to give each of these professionals permission to talk to each other. In the case of an estate with multiple heirs, the settlement process works smoothly when each heir's financial advisor is connected with the others.

In one example, I had a client who was inheriting part of an estate that was being divided among three siblings. One of her siblings had a financial advisor who was near retirement and resisted giving information or returning phone calls. Unable to get information from her, I ended up collaborating with the other sibling's financial advisor, with permission, and we were able to share whatever we could find. Eventually we got the estate sorted out, but it would have been a smoother process with the collaboration of all the advisors.

There are privacy rules that dictate what information can be shared, and a financial advisor will walk you through

what those permissions should look like and the scope of
the information they will ask for or share.

By turning to these professionals for help, and getting
them to speak with each other, you can shift much of the
grunt work of settling a loved one's estate off your shoulders. In part two, you'll see how these professionals can
help you begin constructing your financial future.

FROM PRESENT TO FUTURE: HOW TO INHERIT A NEW FINANCIAL PICTURE

Chapter Four

———

REIMAGINING FINANCIAL GOALS

Angela came to me a year and a half before her husband died. George had Parkinson's, and when I met them, George still held his job at a local hardware store and could still drive. They had already made some decisions: they had downsized to an apartment, so they wouldn't have to take care of a home, and Angela was getting ready to retire early. She knew George would need more and more care as his illness progressed, and she was afraid to leave him home alone.

Angela wanted to understand their finances, and we worked together to streamline their eight retirement accounts and plan their financial road ahead. Taking in the full picture of their income, their expenses, and George's care needs, we evaluated the circumstances to see what Angela could spend sustainably and what decisions made the most sense for them.

The disease was stressful for the couple's daily life, and George's violent behavior strained their relationship with their daughter. When George died, Angela was alone. She laid low and tried to let her wounds heal as much as they could.

Before George died, my work with Angela focused on simplifying their finances. After his death, we were reimagining her financial future. *What did Angela want out of life next? What could her finances support?*

With these questions, we waded into new waters. Angela is fit and likes to hike. She has good friends, but she didn't live near them. We began to focus our financial planning around where she might live and what she might be able to do.

START WITH JOY

When I begin working with a client, I don't just want to know about their finances; I want to know about their whole life.

I start these conversations with lots of questions. I ask about my clients' relationships, families, and activities. These factors influence where they live, how they spend their time, and ultimately, how they spend their money. I ask a variety of questions to understand what is important to them. Some examples include:

- Where does your family live?
- Who is important to you? Where do they live?
- What do you enjoy doing most?
- What keeps you active?
- Where do you like to travel? Who would you like to travel with?
- What kinds of activities would you like to try?

I want to understand where my client found joy before their circumstances changed. We begin to flesh out the parts of their lives that aren't directly connected to the person they lost. Once they can begin to imagine what they want their life to look like, we construct a financial plan to support that future. Money is a tool to support those visions and dreams.

In Angela's case, it took time for her to figure out what she wanted. All of her time leading up to her husband's death was consumed by organizing their finances and dealing with the mounting stress of his illness. After his death, she had a whole new set of decisions to make about how she wanted to live. We worked together to determine what was feasible in her finances, and Angela is considering moving to another state to be near the mountains and her closest friends.

CONNECTING WITH PEOPLE

It's important to recognize how our emotions guide our financial lives. Especially after losing a loved one, our emotions can affect how we see our future and the decisions we make as a result.

I don't recommend making rash, impulsive financial decisions, but after my husband Eric died, my daughter and I went to Disney World twice in one year. The first trip was over my daughter's spring break, and we discovered how stealthy we could be on vacation with just us. There was no negotiating with a group, no need to coordinate with others, and we were able to follow our whims.

Then, just a few weeks later, my sister-in-law said she was taking her kids to Disney. I told her how much fun I'd just had with my daughter and how I wished we could go. Then I stopped myself. We *could* go. It's just us.

I took my daughter out of school, and we went to Disney World again. It was an expensive, impulsive decision, and it was a beautiful way to live on the edge for a moment. We were able to experience joy together.

Losing a loved one can sometimes mean losing connection with friends or family members. A friend told me recently that she lost all of her friends when her husband died, because they were all connections they'd made as a couple. Similarly, I've learned that travel is not a solitary activity for most people, but often when I ask a client who they might like to travel with, they can think of girlfriends, siblings, and other family members that they're interested in connecting with.

Part of the journey after losing a loved one is adjusting your lifestyle to make connections and try new things. A girlfriend and I went to a "paint your pet" night—something I would normally not think to do—and it was hysterical. I don't have an artistic bone in my body, but my friend and I had a great time painting pictures of our pets on canvases.

On this journey into a new lifestyle, we need cheerleaders. Unless a client has a crazy financial decision in mind, I encourage them to follow their wild ideas. Money is a tool to support their visions, dreams, and goals in life.

REDEFINING YOUR RELATIONSHIP TO MONEY

In the firm where I used to work, we used to call the compliance guy "Dr. No" behind his back. His answer to any query was always, "No." Not allowed, *no*.

But there's a balance between living life and being too careful with money. There are certainly tight financial circumstances, and an advisor's goal is to find the lifestyle that your money can support. It's not all about paying the electric bill; there are so many opportunities that don't cost a lot of money but can bring joy and fun to life.

Many people resist seeing a financial advisor because they feel that every time they walk in, they'll be told what they're not doing right. It's like discovering a cavity each time you visit the dentist. No one wants a lecture on brushing and flossing properly with every visit. The better relationship you build with your financial advisor, the more fully they'll see your life and your dreams. Most clients already know the ways they need to be careful with money, and for some clients, I help them see how they could spend a little more.

LET'S TALK NUMBERS

At some point, the discussion of goals and dreams boils down to what you can actually spend now. Many people don't have a clear picture of how much money they spend in a year, and our first step is to look at what their habits are now and put numbers around them.

For some people, tracking every dollar they spend is like asking them to jump off a cliff. In the case of one client, my partner and I worked with her for two years to get her financial plan done, but she hemmed and hawed over tracking her finances. Finally, I asked her to figure out what her income was, subtract how much she'd saved, and we could figure out what she'd spent. She came up with a number, and it surprised her. We were looking forward to her future: with a husband twenty years her senior, she was heading toward a transition. She needed to plan for losing his Social Security benefit upon his death and how that would shift her spending.

Sometimes in this deeper look at finances, you might discover that it's necessary to make adjustments to your lifestyle. Around the time my husband Eric died, a new client came to see me whose husband had just died. He managed all the money and may have even given her an overly optimistic view of their finances. She would ask her husband if they were financially secure, and he would say yes. She accepted that. After his death, she had been impulsive in her shopping. If you asked her what she'd spent money on, she wouldn't be able to say. When her husband was alive, he probably spent more than he should have as well. Together, they had a habit of spending that wasn't sustainable in the long run.

This client wasn't able to see her situation until we started pulling her financial pieces together. Just because someone doesn't know their financial situation doesn't mean it's a bad one, but that knowledge creates a crucial context for financial decisions. Knowing your assets and your expenses is pivotal for understanding what financial strategies support your lifestyle.

In my own situation, losing my husband Eric came not only with a huge emotional loss but with a loss of income as well. We had been in the middle of renovating our home, and our financial plans had been built around both of our incomes. With this financial loss, certain elements of settling his affairs, such as addressing his life insurance policy, became more urgent than they otherwise would have been.

In the wake of a loss, each piece that you can resolve allows some of the emotional burden to be unloaded as well. With each step, you get a little bit closer to your new normal. In the same way, planning your own financial future can help you get a clear view of the lifestyle your finances will support.

Financial plans are built from the bottom up. First, we

pull out the biggest expenses. What does it take to keep the lights on, food on the table, and maintain medical insurance? What other fixed expenses are in your financial picture?

From there, we add on goals and desires that aren't requirements. How much travel do you want to do? What activities do you want to pursue? We make a list of goals and discuss the financial plan that would truly represent the future you want.

We start solving for discrepancies. Given your set of circumstances, does this financial picture work? If your spending isn't where you want it, what can we do to change that? Can you give up on one side of your spending to make something else a reality? The greatest value of a financial advisor is in giving perspective to see what we can do differently.

Lastly, we consider the assumptions at play in your financial plan. Following the current numbers in your income and expenses requires a set of assumptions: we assume you're going to work until a certain age and live to a certain age, and we assume inflation will rise at a particular rate and your investments will have an estimated rate of return. Layered on top of all these assumptions is the possibility that they may play out differently. What if you don't keep your job to age sixty-five? What if your spouse dies at age seventy, but you live to be ninety? Financial planning is a tool to develop a frame of reference, and it allows us to set expectations for what is sustainable in the long term.

MINDSETS AROUND INHERITANCE

Often, when clients inherit money they didn't earn themselves, I see a higher degree of fear that the money will disappear and they'll have no way to replace it. One of my clients inherited money from an aunt, and as we began making plans with it, she was unwilling to spend it. Though she and her husband had no children or heirs they wanted to leave the money to, she felt responsibility to hold onto her aunt's money.

She's not alone. I've seen many clients become more protective of the money they inherit than the money they earn. This makes our planning conversations more difficult. We begin our planning by treating inherited money as available funds, but if they're not willing to spend it, we have to take it out of their plan. They have a tough time reconciling that these savings are there to support their lives.

GOALS IN CHAOS

Losing a loved one, or planning for a loved one's incapacity, can change one's goals and visions dramatically. Sometimes it's not about imagining *what if* but about identifying *what is*. What is the reality of this new financial picture? In the case of losing a spouse, this can often mean losing significant income and coming into a new understanding about what will support your financial future.

Sometimes, a financial plan is less about living one's dreams and more about setting up the care that the finances can support. In the case of my brother-in-law Stan, our first steps were to figure out what his options were for a living arrangement. We considered family members he could live with or people we could hire for his care, and we found the estate could support him moving to an assisted living facility.

Part of planning care for a family member is ensuring that the money can cover long-term care for the rest of a person's life, as well as the higher degrees of care they will need as they age. It can easily cost over $100,000 per year for nursing care and enrichment in a shared-room facility. The average length of stay in these facilities is three years, but what if it stretches to six or seven? Once we've identified these possible futures, we can set up an investment plan to give the best chance to support those scenarios.

There is no silver bullet to prepare for incapacity or an

uncertain medical and financial future. By taking your current financial picture into account along with the possibilities you face, you can take small steps to prepare the best you can.

LET YOUR GOALS GUIDE YOU

Your financial goals aren't static; they change in response to the stages and events of your life. Taking time to revisit your goals after a tragedy can help you manage the chaos and set up a clearer financial picture for the future.

In the next chapter, we'll start to see how these goals translate into practical steps in handling the accounts you might inherit (or create for yourself). We'll define the various types of retirement accounts and how inheriting one might change your financial picture.

Chapter Five

INHERITING ACCOUNTS

When Carol walked into my office, she was fried. She must have finished a cigarette right before coming in. She smelled of smoke, and she looked like she'd just been through a wind tunnel. My heart went out to her. She was a piano teacher, and numbers didn't come naturally to her. Now, here she was in my office holding shopping bags full of papers. She dumped them all on my desk.

Together, we began sorting through them. She had kept all the notifications she'd received, however small. I started peeling through and pitching the papers we didn't need (*"This mutual fund is changing its name to..."*) and putting statements from the same account together. Then I could see where she stood.

One of the papers was a year-end account statement for a beneficiary IRA.

"Do you know you're supposed to be taking a distribution on this account?" I asked. There was no distribution listed on the statement.

Her face dropped. "What do you mean?"

I explained what I saw: she had inherited an account from her mother, and the insurance company that controlled it had set up the account correctly in Carol's name. She'd likely received a letter when the new account was opened that would have explained that Carol would be required to take distributions from the account once a year. Carol had either missed the letter, or she didn't understand it. In the ten years since the account had been opened, she'd never been contacted to see why she wasn't taking her distribution.

As you'll see in this chapter, inherited accounts have varying rules about how distributions must be managed. These distributions have huge tax implications, and there are big tax penalties if you don't take them when you're supposed to.

Here Carol was, realizing ten years later that she was supposed to have this distribution on her tax return every year. This was a monster of a mess.

We called the insurance company together, and we tried to talk to the broker. They were very uncooperative. They refused to take responsibility for not having contacted Carol or helping her understand what she needed to do.

In the end, she needed a professional to help her sort out the question of her taxes. I got her accounts as organized as I could and referred her to an accountant.

Because distributions can have a large impact on taxes, it's important to have a strategy for when to take them. When you stretch distributions over a longer period of time, the growth of those investments can offset the tax that is paid each time you take a distribution. When distributions are taken very quickly in large sums, you not only pay the tax on that lump sum, but you miss out on the opportunity for the investment to grow.

For example, if someone inherited an IRA account worth $100,000, and they took a distribution on this lump sum all at once, they would pay around 25 percent in taxes. They would end up with roughly $75,000. However, if the heir took the minimum distribution—we'll use $2,000 for our example—they would leave the remaining $98,000 in the portfolio to grow over the next year. They would be taxed on the $2,000 distribution they receive, but that amount would easily be surpassed in growth: if the remaining $98,000 grew at 5 percent, the heir would have $102,000 in their portfolio after one year. By taking distributions over a longer period of time, it's possible to rebuild the coffers and cover the amount of tax paid on smaller distributions.

In contrast to Carol, I had another client with a complicated estate who wouldn't name the beneficiaries on his retirement account despite my urgings that he do so. There is a rule that states that when no beneficiary is named on a retirement account, the money must be distributed within five years of the account owner's death. When this client died, his children were forced to take their distributions a lot faster than I would typically recommend, and they took big tax hits on their inheritances. When larger distributions are taken quickly, there is less money in the account to grow, and it's harder to make up the total hit from distribution and taxes. The children ended up keeping around 70 percent of the assets from their father's estate and losing about 30 percent to taxes.

This is why it is so important to understand what accounts you're working with. Each account has unique rules for how it is managed and distributed. Now that your papers are organized with like accounts together, we'll take a look at what you need to know about each type of account.

BASIC ACCOUNT TYPES

From individual retirement accounts (IRAs) to taxable accounts, there are many ways to save and grow assets and set them up to be inherited after death. In this section, we'll define each of the major account types: taxable accounts, traditional and Roth IRAs, employer plans, and annuities.

"Beneficiary IRA" refers to an IRA that's been inherited (this is also called an Inherited IRA). The inherited account maintains the same character as the original. For example, if a traditional IRA was left to an heir, that account converts to a beneficiary IRA with the same tax structures as the original IRA. The distribution rules change when an account is inherited, and we'll cover the differences in each of the sections below. Each of these account types has a different tax status, distribution rules, and barriers to access.

TAXABLE ACCOUNTS

A taxable account is an investment account that allows you to grow your assets without the restrictions of a retirement account. Contributions to retirement accounts are tax-deferred, meaning that money is put into these accounts before income tax is applied. In contrast, contributions to taxable accounts are made after income taxes have been paid, which makes these accounts far more flexible. You can invest in stocks and mutual funds to grow your money, and there are no barriers to taking money out of taxable accounts. There are also no limits to how much money you can put in.

Tax Implications

Taxable accounts are subject to two types of tax. The first is capital gains tax. Let's say you buy a stock for one hundred dollars, and three years later, you sell it for $500. The $400 growth gets taxed as income, but it's treated at the capital gains tax rate. At 15 percent, this capital gains tax rate is lower than most people's income tax rate, which ranges from 10 percent to 37 percent.

The second tax is a tax on your dividends, or your interest. Income from dividends is reported as normal income and taxed at your regular income tax rate. In this dual tax identity, the capital gains tax on growth is typically the larger part of the tax you pay on a taxable account. The taxes on gains and losses only come into play when you've actually sold an investment. We'll discuss capital gains and dividends in more depth in the next chapter on investments.

If you sell stock at a loss, you can use that loss to reduce your income. There are some minutiae with these strategies, but as a basic example, if you have a $500 gain on one stock and a $500 loss on another, they offset each other, and there's zero impact on your taxes. There is a limit to how much loss you can report on your taxes each year: $3,000. Let's say you took a $30,000 loss one year but didn't sell other stocks at a gain. In that example, you could claim $3,000 of that loss per year on your taxes to reduce your taxable income. A loss like this can become a valuable tax planning tool, even if you're not making money on a taxable account.

If you're fortunate enough to have money to save beyond what you're putting into your retirement accounts, a taxable account is a great way to grow your wealth and maintain access to use your wealth toward your goals.

Distribution Rules

While inheriting a retirement account comes with rules about when you need to take distributions, there are no rules of distribution for inheriting a taxable account.

When taxable accounts are inherited, they receive a *step up in cost basis*. The *cost basis* of an investment is the original amount paid for the stock. When the stock grows and its value changes after purchase, the *gain* is the difference between the original amount paid and the present-day amount after growth. When the cost basis "steps up," the base value of the stock becomes the current-day value on the date of death.

As an example, let's say your grandparent bought Ford stock fifty years ago when it was three dollars per share. Today, it's worth sixty dollars per share. If you were to sell that stock, there would be a huge capital gain tax waiting for you. However, the *step up in cost basis* means that the stock's value on the day of death becomes the new cost basis. The capital gains tax would no longer be calculated off the three dollars per share from your grandparent's day, but rather from the sixty dollars per share value when you inherited it. The huge capital gain tax gets wiped away. You now own the stock, and when you sell it, your gains will be calculated by how much it grew from the sixty dollars per share price on the day you inherited it.

This means that inheriting stock in a taxable account creates a beautiful opportunity to diversify investments. You have a lot of flexibility to sell. Before you do, it's important to make sure that the account value is properly stepped up in cost basis. The institution handling the account can take care of this easily, and they'll need a copy of the death certificate, so they have the date of death to calculate the new cost basis. They won't step up the cost basis automatically, however, so it's important to make sure the step up is documented before you sell an inherited stock.

TRADITIONAL IRAS

This type of account is set up specifically to save and invest money for retirement. The tax structure and distribution rules of traditional IRAs are designed to grow wealth long term and discourage taking money out before retirement age.

Tax Implications

When you make contributions to a traditional IRA, you receive a tax deduction. However, there is a limit to how much you can contribute to this type of account per year. As of this writing, it's $6,000 if you're under fifty, and $7,000 if you're over fifty.

Not only do you get a tax deduction for putting money into an IRA, but once money is invested in the account, it grows tax deferred, meaning you don't pay taxes on those funds in the time that you hold the investment. The money in an IRA continues to grow and grow, and taxes are taken only when you take money out as a distribution.

Distribution Rules

Because money in an IRA is intended for retirement, penalties apply if you take money out before the age of fifty-nine and a half. Standard federal and state taxes apply if you take distributions early, and additionally, a

10 percent penalty will be taken from the value of the distribution. In all, this adds up to about a 45 percent loss of value to taxes.

Once you hit age fifty-nine and a half, you can take as much or as little distribution as you want, and you'll pay federal and state income taxes on what you receive. As you know from the previous section, income taxes are higher for most people than the capital gains tax rate, so it's good to have a mix of taxable accounts and IRAs to preserve and grow your wealth.

From age seventy and a half on, you are required to take a minimum distribution from your IRA, as calculated by a federal formula.

When inheriting an IRA, there are a few quirks to the distribution rules, depending on how the heir handles the account they receive.

When a spouse inherits an IRA, they have the option to treat the IRA as their own, and this comes with its own unique rules. In this case, the spouse would designate themselves as the new account owner, and they can continue to manage and contribute to the account. The distribution requirement is based on the age of the person who died, not the person who inherits the account. This means that if one spouse died at the age of sixty, but the surviving spouse is fifty-five, the surviving spouse could start taking the distribution penalty-free because the deceased spouse was at the age to qualify. It also means that the clock continues for when the minimum distribution requirement kicks in. When the deceased spouse would have turned seventy and a half, the surviving spouse is required to take out minimum distributions from that point forward.

This time period, between when distributions are *allowed* (beginning at age fifty-nine and a half) to when they are *required* (at age seventy and a half) is a "freedom zone." Based on how the surviving spouse wishes to take distributions in this range—and whether they want to calculate distributions off their spouse's age or their own—a surviving spouse may choose to treat the deceased spouse's IRA as their own, or to transfer the funds to their own account.

Transferring the funds into a new account in the surviving spouse's name can be a useful way to reset the distribution rules. In an example with one client, her older spouse died, and she was required to take distributions that were much higher than she would normally take for herself. She didn't need the money, and this resulted in her paying higher taxes than she needed to. We changed the account into her name, so that the standard IRA distribution rules would apply based on her age, not her husband's. Transferring an inherited IRA into a surviving spouse's account relieves the tax burden of the distributions and gives the heir freedom to wait until age seventy and a half to begin taking money out.

Lastly, survivors who aren't spouses need to create an Inherited IRA from the deceased's account. Spouses can take this option as well, and, depending on how they would like their distributions structured, it may be a better option than creating a new account in their name. The minimum required distribution that a beneficiary must take from an Inherited IRA is very specific and dependent on the beneficiary's age. This figure is calculated with a table from the IRS called the Single Life Table for Inherited IRAs, and it is determined by the beneficiary's age at the time of inheritance, adjusting with their age throughout their lifetime. The table can be found on the IRS website, and a financial advisor or investment broker can help you calculate the exact amount you're required to take if you've inherited an IRA.

ROTH IRAS

A Roth IRA is a different animal from a traditional IRA. It has a unique tax treatment and no required distributions until inherited, which make this type of account a lovely legacy planning tool to pass down to heirs.

Tax Implications

Like a taxable account, you do not get a tax deduction for contributing to a Roth IRA; money is put into this type of account after income tax has been applied. The limits to how much you can contribute are the same as a traditional IRA: $6,000 per year, or $7,000 per year after the age of fifty. The genius and beauty of a Roth IRA is that money in this type of account grows tax-deferred just like it would in a traditional IRA, but when money is distributed from a Roth IRA, there is no tax on the distribution.

Distribution Rules

Similar to a taxable account, there is no required distribution from a Roth IRA. You must be fifty-nine and a half to take distributions from a Roth IRA without penalty, and additionally, the account has to have been open (though not necessarily funded) for at least five years before taking a distribution.

When a Roth IRA is inherited, the heir can stretch distributions out over their lifetime, and they don't pay taxes on the money they receive. There are also no penalties for taking money out early when the account is inherited.

EMPLOYER-SPONSORED RETIREMENT ACCOUNTS

There are several kinds of retirement accounts that can

be accessed through an employer or a business. A few of the more common account types include:

- **401(k):** Like a traditional IRA, when you contribute money to a 401(k), you receive a tax deduction, the money grows tax-deferred, and the distribution rules and taxes are the same. The crucial difference is that the contribution limits are much higher for a 401(k). As of this writing, people under the age of fifty can contribute up to $19,000 per year, and people over fifty can contribute $25,000 per year. These contributions come straight off an employee's paycheck. Additionally, most companies match an employee's contributions up to a percentage of the employee's salary (usually between 3–6 percent). This means that if you contribute 3 percent of your yearly income to your 401(k), your employer would put in the same amount of money you do. This type of account is designed to build assets.
- **Savings Incentive Match Plan for Employees (SIMPLE) plans, Solo 401(k)s, and Defined Benefit Plans:** These plans are typically used by self-employed people to put money aside for retirement on a tax-deferred basis (though they can also be used by large corporations to set up pension plans). Larger contributions are allowed in these types of accounts than in standard, traditional IRAs. Like other retirement plans, these accounts have penalties for early

withdrawal, as well as distribution requirements. Owners of these funds have a variety of options for how payouts are distributed; for example, they can elect to have a percentage of their payout go to a spouse. These elections also affect the way those funds are inherited. If you're setting up a defined-benefit plan, it's important to know the elections available to you, and a financial advisor can guide you to make the elections that match your needs.

- **Simplified Employee Pension (SEP):** This is another type of self-employed retirement plan, with the same contribution limits as a traditional IRA, at $6,000 (up to age fifty) and $7,000 (over age fifty). Business contributions can be higher on a SEP plan.
- **403(b), 457, and variations:** These plans function the same way that 401(k) plans do, but they are set up for government employees and educational institutions. They allow much higher contributions than SIMPLE and SEP plans, and they are eligible for matches from an employer.

Distribution Rules

The distribution rules for employer-sponsored retirement accounts are the same as for an IRA.

When these accounts are inherited, they usually get transferred into a traditional IRA. This allows for the heir to plan and manage their account without going through their loved one's employer. Employers may have limited options for investments, and they may require you to go through their human resources department to make any changes or distributions. Additionally, there are usually fees associated with these accounts. While the employee holds the plan, the corporation or the employee are responsible for the costs of administering the plan, but an heir may have to cover all the costs of an inherited plan themselves.

For these reasons, it's more favorable to transfer these accounts into IRAs and consolidate assets into whichever custodian you prefer. This gives you investment choices, greater control, and no need to go through an HR department. If an inherited account is performing well, you can typically transfer this account into your own Inherited IRA and still redistribute it in the same way to continue the same performance. Most 401(k)s, however, tend to be a bit of a mess because the employee choosing their investment options often doesn't have the expertise to select a balanced portfolio. You'll learn more about what to look for in a portfolio and how to balance your investment mix in the next chapter.

ANNUITIES

An annuity is an insurance contract for an investment.

Annuities can be part of an investment plan within an IRA, and they have the same distribution rules as an IRA. However, they can have additional barriers to access the investments, called "surrender periods," usually seven to ten years long, that restrict when you can take money out of these accounts. During the surrender period there are "surrender charges," which are additional monetary penalties for taking money out of the account.

There are appropriate times to use annuities in an investment portfolio, but I sometimes see clients who were pushed into high-commission annuities that trapped their investments.

In one case, my client Barb inherited money from her mother in the form of a taxable account, but she didn't know what to do with the money. A broker sold her an annuity. Barb didn't understand the distribution rules and tax treatments around this product, and she essentially locked the money away from herself for several years because of the surrender charge. When Barb came to me, we discovered that there was a high fee structure on her annuity, which meant that the growth of her investments was stunted. She wasn't seeing the amount of growth she wanted to compensate for the fees on the account.

Although she was very frugal with her money, Barb

needed her mother's inheritance to complete renovations to her house, but she couldn't access it. To improve her access to the money, we rolled this account into a low-fee annuity with no surrender charge. She still didn't have great access to the money, but we could take out a little bit at a time without inflating her income too much with the gains on her growth. It took about five years to get out of the annuity without destroying her tax returns.

Often, scenarios like Barb's happen because clients are overwhelmed with grief. Barb had made her initial decision to buy the annuity because she thought she needed to act fast with her mother's money, and it was difficult to take the proper time and consideration to understand what she was buying. A client's internal compass may tell them something is off, but they don't know what else to do. Annuities can be particularly tricky financial products because their fee structures and rules are so variable.

It's important to be able to clearly understand the fees, distribution requirements, and tax structure of your investments. Because an annuity is a contract for an investment with an insurance company, each contract stipulates the particulars of that purchase. Below we'll cover some of the general guidelines, but if you're considering including an annuity in your investments, it's important to understand the fine print of your contract.

Distribution Rules

Annuities come in two types: variable and fixed. With fixed annuities, the owner has a guaranteed, fixed monthly income once they start taking distributions. For example, you may pay $500,000 into an annuity in exchange for receiving a fixed $5,000 payment per month for the rest of your life. Usually with fixed annuities, when the owner dies, the policy dies with them; those payments are not passed on to an heir. If only $60,000 of the $500,000 was paid out over the owner's lifetime, the company holding the annuity keeps the remainder. Because of this, fixed annuities are typically not inherited.

However, there are many different ways to set up an annuity, and some of those structures can be passed on. For example, if a loved one has purchased a product called a "ten-year certain," the insurance company will continue to pay the owner or their beneficiary the fixed payment for ten years.

Variable annuities function much more like traditional IRAs, with the same age requirements for distributions. It's also possible to buy after-tax annuities, which have looser requirements for when money can be taken out. As the name implies, money is paid into after-tax annuities after income tax is taken out. When distributions are taken, taxes are applied only to the growth of the investments. This gives these after-tax annuities more flexibility in their distribution rules. The annuity's specific contract will stipulate the terms for when distributions can be taken and when penalties apply.

HOW INHERITANCE AFFECTS MARITAL ASSETS

When you're married, any wealth you accrue in joint accounts is considered equally owned by both spouses.

When you inherit assets from outside the marriage (for example, from the parent of one spouse), you face the choice to keep that inherited asset in your name or create a joint account for it with your spouse. Once you put it into a joint account, you've gifted that asset to the marriage.

In most cases, it's important to keep these kinds of inheritances separate. Should you go through a divorce with those assets in a joint account, they are considered a marital asset and are split. If you inherit an account and keep it in your own name, it never becomes subject to division from a divorce.

When a spouse dies, jointly-owned property becomes solely owned by the surviving spouse. This affects investments in a taxable account in a unique way because, as you'll recall from earlier, inherited investments receive a step up in cost basis. On a jointly-owned taxable account, the surviving spouse would receive a step up in cost basis on the deceased's half of the investments. This means that if a couple jointly owns one hundred shares of IBM stock in a taxable account, the surviving spouse would receive a step up in cost basis on fifty of those shares. As in the case of an heir inheriting a taxable account, the step up in cost basis is not automatic; the surviving spouse would need to contact the institution holding the stock to request the step up on the deceased's half of the account. This can be done any time before the stock is sold.

NAMING YOUR BENEFICIARIES

When you're opening your own IRAs or transferring assets from a loved one's account, it's important to name a beneficiary of your own, so that your assets can be inherited easily in the event of your death. As we discussed in chapter 1, naming your beneficiary is a simple step in the account set-up process, and you should check every year that your beneficiary designation is up to date. After death, it's not possible to change the beneficiary that is recorded on the account, so taking a moment to review this each year will ensure that your assets are inherited as you intend.

A GOLDEN OPPORTUNITY

Inheriting any account comes with a set of requirements:

it's important to understand how distributions should be taken and what strategy fits your goals best. Inheriting an account also creates a golden opportunity to create the right financial plans to serve your vision for the future. In the next chapter, we'll take a look at the investments inside these accounts. You'll see how investment trends influenced the accounts you've inherited, and we'll lay out the basics for a balanced portfolio, so you can understand how to evaluate your investments for your own needs.

Chapter Six

———

UNDERSTANDING INVESTMENTS

I met Bethany while she was caring for her aunt in the final years of her aunt's life. Bethany came to me to help manage her aunt's money, which was originally all invested in one hotel stock. The aunt had been forced to liquidate the investment when the hotel chain was purchased, and that's when Bethany came to me. The aunt's previous strategy fit a pattern I'd seen in her generation, where only a few stocks are held in a portfolio, without much diversity. Reinvesting the aunt's hotel stock was hugely beneficial to making sure the money would carry her through several years of intense nursing care.

It was clear that the aunt's care wasn't convenient or fun, and Bethany did an amazing job making sure all her bills were paid and her estate was arranged. When the aunt died several years later, the estate was divided between Bethany and her brother.

Additionally, Bethany's father had moved into assisted living, and Bethany kept an eye on things, including his finances. When her father died, that estate was again divided between Bethany and her brother. Bethany lived a very frugal lifestyle, and she made a very generous plan with these two inheritances: she decided to set her father's estate aside to be an inheritance for her own nieces and nephews. As for her aunt's estate, she planned to very cautiously and wisely spend every penny of it to support her own dreams.

We sold everything in the portfolio that did not fit with Bethany's strategy, and we invested those assets according to her goals. The possibilities of what she could do with her life shifted with this inheritance. Bethany and her husband began looking to buy a new house. Beyond that, the inheritance gave her more freedom to choose how and when she wanted to work, which opened up her leisure time.

So often, the investments we inherit were designed for our loved one's goals, but they don't fit our own. It can be emotionally difficult to sell all the investments you inherit, but there's a unique opportunity shortly after inheritance to customize the investment profile to fit your goals. This opportunity centers around the step up in cost basis.

A STEP UP

As you recall from the last chapter, the original cost basis of stock is the price per share when it was purchased. Over time, the share price of that company fluctuates and generally trends upward as the company grows. When you inherit a stock, the cost basis is reset to the cost of the share on the date of death. The heir never has to pay taxes on the growth of the stock from its original cost basis to the "step up" in cost basis when it is reset. This rule presents a wonderful advantage to reinvest assets into a portfolio that is tailored to your needs.

HOW INVESTMENTS GENERATE WEALTH

Before we dive into how to create a portfolio of balanced investments, it's important to understand how stocks, bonds, and mutual funds grow wealth. With an understanding of these products, you can begin to assess what investments might be right for you.

STOCKS

When you own stock in a company, what you actually own

is equity in that business. Some people perceive the stock market as the "Wall Street casino," but it's not gambling—when you own a share of a company, its profitability has a direct impact on you. For example, if a company has a hundred shares of stock, and you own ten of them, you're a 10 percent owner of the company. You have a participatory interest. As a part owner, you receive shares of that company's profits.

There are two components of a stock that generate wealth. The first is through dividends, and the second is the growth of the stock price over the principal (that is, over what you paid for it). Together, these make up your total returns. We'll take a look at each of these components individually.

Dividends

After a corporation has paid all their expenses to operate, they have two choices for what to do with their leftover profit. They may choose to invest that profit back into the company to fuel future growth, such as buying new equipment or paying bonuses to their workers. Or, they may choose to pay that profit out to shareholders. This profit payout is a dividend.

Dividends tend to be stable, and they tend to increase over time. When investors receive a consistent dividend, they have a perceived guarantee: this income is often steady even if the stock market price fluctuates. In turn, the stock price tends to stabilize when investors are confident in their returns.

Dividends don't always last. In 2008, at the height of the recession, many companies cut their dividends drastically. Wells Fargo, for example, reduced their dividend by 85 percent. Ford took their dividends all the way to zero—a big risk, as it could influence investors to sell their shares. As big companies needed more cash internally, they couldn't afford to pay out profits to shareholders. Investors who lived off their dividends were hit hard by their companies' cutbacks. Market conditions like this have shaped investors' attitudes and behaviors over time, so that different generations of people often have different strategies for their investments (more on that in the next section).

Large market swings aside, dividends tend to be the more stable component of the income investors see in their returns, and this drives investors' decisions about which stocks to choose.

Principal and Growth

The second way that stocks generate wealth is through the growth of the stock price. How much return you see from that growth depends on what you paid for the stock (the principal) and when you decide to sell the stock. The profit you make from selling the stock at a higher price than you purchased it is called the capital gain. As noted in the previous chapter, capital gains are taxed at a lower rate than most people's income tax rate, making them an attractive tool to grow wealth.

Often what drives changes in stock prices is the public perception of how that stock will perform in the future. A stock rises or falls with how confident people are in that company's ability to make long-term profits.

Shareholders base their confidence on the company's performance and, even more specifically, their ability to innovate. We can see these influences play out in the history of Pfizer stock. The pressure pharmaceutical companies experience to produce new drugs is impacted by two factors. First, the research and development phase for creating new drugs is a long process, as new drugs go through clinical trials after they are produced. Second, pharmaceutical companies hold patents on their drugs for only a set period of time, after which generics can be made, drastically cutting the profits of the name-brand drug. Because of these factors, pharmaceutical companies rely on "blockbuster" drugs to turn a large profit in the short years between their release and the expiration of their patents.

Pfizer had a string of blockbuster drugs in the '80s and '90s, and stock prices climbed swiftly, peaking with the success of drugs like Lipitor and Viagra. This primed the expectation of shareholders that Pfizer would continue to climb at the same rate with new, innovative drugs continuing to hit the market. However, Pfizer didn't deliver. In the 2000s, Pfizer stock began to fall: as patents on their flagship drugs expired, their new innovations didn't perform strongly enough to match shareholder expectations. After buying several other pharmaceutical companies, Pfizer's stock price rebounded in the last decade with new drugs performing well once more.

In this example, we see clearly that stock price is impacted by the company's innovation and how well their performance matches shareholder expectations. When a company cannot deliver innovation to the degree that is expected, the stock price is negatively impacted.

Information about a company's stock price, their innovation initiatives, their sales, and the strength of their competitors is publicly available, so everyone who participates in the market has access to information about the company's health and growth potential. As a result, stock prices tend to be fairly close to the reality of what a company's share is worth because there is so much information to inform market participants' decisions to buy and sell.

However, we can see some examples where stock price is driven above the value of a company's earnings because shareholders believe in the future growth of the company. Amazon is a primary example: they have a lot of revenue, and they've reinvested much of it into growing other parts of their business. Amazon doesn't have high earnings that could potentially become distributions for shareholders, but their stock price is huge. People predict that Amazon's investments in its future growth will pay off and make the company more valuable, so they're willing to pay a higher price for the stock. This pushes the stock price up, even though the actual earnings of the company aren't high enough to support the stock price.

It's not all guesswork. How companies like Amazon reinvest their revenue is reported publicly, so shareholders can evaluate those plays and make investment decisions based on how they think the company's developments will pay off.

These perceptions not only shape the fluctuations of today's stock market, but they also influence the strategies that previous generations have used to invest.

BONDS

While a stock is a share of ownership in a company, a bond is a loan to a company or institution. The investor purchases the bond at face value, and they receive a fixed interest rate on the loan. Interest payments are typically issued annually or broken into two payments per year. The investor continues to receive these interest payments until the bond's maturity date. At that point, the face value of the loan is paid back to the investor.

One of the largest borrowers is the US government, though companies can also issue bonds. In a low interest rate environment, bonds can be a cheap way to fund an operation, especially if the company can grow faster than the interest rate on their loans.

Bonds are more stable than stocks because you know what the payoff is going to be. If you buy a bond that promises a 3 percent interest rate for ten years, you know exactly how much you'll get in interest, as well as the date of maturity when you'll be fully repaid.

While a bond's interest rate is fixed at the time of purchase, market interest rates fluctuate over time. This means that the market value of a particular bond also fluctuates if it was purchased at a higher or lower rate than the prevailing interest rate.

Let's look at an example with a US government bond. Imagine an investor buys a ten-year government bond for $10,000 at 5 percent interest. The interest rate is fixed, so for ten years, the investor will receive $500 per year in interest payments. If the interest rate drops to 3 percent a few years later, a new investor purchasing a similar $10,000 bond will only receive $300 per year. Both investors paid for the same face value, and both will receive their $10,000 back after the maturity date, but the first investor makes more money in interest.

When investors decide to sell their bonds before the maturity date, the selling price is influenced by the current interest rate, as well as the fixed interest rate of the bond. In our above example, the investor who owns the 5 percent bond would charge a premium because their bond is more valuable than the market rate. A buyer would then pay extra to receive the higher interest payments for the rest of the life of the bond. Conversely, if an investor wanted to sell a bond whose interest rate was below the prevailing interest rate, they would sell at a discount to make up for the lower value of the bond. The buyer would pay less for the bond, and receive lower interest payments, but they would still receive the full face value of the bond when it matures.

The stability of bonds makes them an anchor for a portfolio. The downsides to bonds are that they're less liquid (that is, converting them into cash quickly can be more difficult than with stocks), they grow at a slower rate than stocks, and the amount you receive back is fixed even if the company's growth exceeds expectations. The biggest risk with a bond is bankruptcy: should the company collapse and default on their loans, lenders won't receive their money back. This risk is rare, and it's mitigated by rating agencies, such as the Standard & Poor's Index and Moody's Corporation, that determine the investment quality of bonds. These institutions rate bonds on a scale from AAA (highest) to CCC (lowest). Bonds with a rating of BBB or lower are considered "junk bonds" that are below investment grade, meaning the company is not stable enough to make their bond a reliable investment.

With their reliable payoffs and low risk, bonds are a good tool for diversity in an investment portfolio.

MUTUAL FUNDS

Mutual funds are a formal way to group stocks, bonds, or a mixture of both. When you invest in a mutual fund, you're not buying stock directly. Instead, you put money into the fund, your money is grouped with other investors, and the fund manager invests this money according to the fund's mandate. For example, if you invest in a Large Cap US mutual fund, the manager chooses large companies in the US in which to buy stock. You then own percentages of stocks in all the companies that make up that fund. When managed wisely, a mutual fund is a vehicle to get a lot of diversification from one investment.

When holding several mutual funds, it's important to understand the mandate directing the investments of each one. You could have several funds with similar diversification strategies, making the sum total of these investments less diversified than they seem.

GENERATIONAL SHIFTS

It's not uncommon to come across older people with singular investment strategies like Bethany's aunt, who held all of her stocks in a single hotel chain. Often, our investment plans are guided by how much we trust the companies and institutions that we've put our money into. Many people in older generations were affected by the Great Depression. There are many people in that generation who wouldn't buy stocks at all, and some people even developed a mistrust of banks. I have several clients whose parents have cash stuck in places all over their houses; they felt their money was safer and easier to access in their home than in an institution.

In a financial climate like the one endured after the Great Depression, if you're going to buy stock, who can you trust? For older generations, the answer was often in larger companies, like Ford, that had public visibility. Others bought stock at the companies where they worked because they were familiar with the company's operations and its growth. Another guiding mentality was to look for the companies that would pay the largest dividends and create seemingly reliable income.

But as we saw when dividends plummeted in the wake of the Great Recession, strategies that worked in past markets may not be appropriate in the current financial climate. Similarly, investment strategies that supported the goals of your loved one may not support your vision for the future. The key is to regularly evaluate your investment portfolio and adjust it based on how it's performing for you.

A BALANCED PORTFOLIO

The first indicator a financial advisor looks at in a portfolio is the overall mix of stocks and bonds. A generic starting point is a 60/40 ratio of stocks to bonds, but the particulars of this mix will be different for each individual, depending on their personal goals and their risk tolerance.

To determine what that should look like, we ask a lot of questions about the investments they've made in the past and their future needs. *When do you expect to need the money you're investing? How comfortable are you with seeing stock values fluctuate on your statements? How much have you saved, and how much time do you have for your money to grow?* It's important to place the client's current needs in the context of their financial history and future plans, so we can see how they'll need their investments to perform for the future.

For example, if a client knows they'll need to cash out their investments within five years, stocks aren't the best investment vehicle for them. If there's a short-term downturn in the market, those investments will need time to recover and grow.

On the other hand, if a client has plenty of time and a small amount of savings, we may want to consider stretching their comfort zone with a larger proportion of stocks to maximize their growth. When making these decisions, we always consider each client's comfort level with their risk.

Put simply, risk tolerance is your ability to sleep at night when the markets go down. It's never a good idea to sell into a down market, and you'll need to balance that rule against the worry and anxiety you might feel as you weather a dip in your investment values.

MARKET CORRECTIONS

Fluctuations in the stock market are caused by the collective moves of market participants buying and selling their stocks. These shifts between buyers and sellers determine the fair prices of stocks. When stock prices creep higher than the underlying value of the corporation, market participants begin to sell, and this can result in a "market correction" to bring the price back down.

The Great Recession presents a dramatic example. In 2008, stock prices soared because of euphoric spending as many people bought houses they couldn't afford. Housing markets tend to feed other stocks because as people buy new houses, they buy more stuff (think of all the trips to Lowe's for home repairs and improvements).

The housing market collapsed under several forces. Potential homeowners were not required to pay down payments, and they could secure loans with variable rates that offered small payments at the start. When those loans reset after the first few years, mortgage payments jumped, and some homeowners could no longer afford their houses. People began defaulting on their loans. If the defaulting homeowner hadn't built equity—if, for example, they'd bought their house without a down payment—they lost value on their home and owed money when they sold it. This negatively impacted the major financial institutions that held these loans, and it created ripple effects across the stock market. Investors saw that the euphoric spending in the housing market wasn't sustainable, and they pulled out of their investments, resulting in a further downturn in the market.

You can't prevent a market correction, but you can prevent a portfolio from experiencing more of a hit than necessary. In assessing the mix of stocks and bonds in a portfolio, it's important to account for how much time you'll have before you need to take money out of the market to spend.

If you have a high percentage of stock in your portfolio when you begin taking distributions, you become more vulnerable to fluctuations in the market. If you need to take money out of the market during a downturn, you do long-term damage to your portfolio. Not only have you temporarily lost value in the stocks you liquidate, but you also lose the opportunity to grow that money. When the markets do turn around, you have a lower base of investments to grow. Historically, stock prices recover from market corrections in three years or less.

As you can see, you want to avoid taking distributions from investments in the middle of a market correction, so it's important to balance your portfolio based on how soon you may need money back out of the market. Stocks are the best vehicle for growth in a portfolio, and a mix of bonds are used to mitigate the volatility of the markets, particularly as you take distributions from your investments.

Another tool for weathering market corrections is to invest in different kinds of markets.

INTERNATIONAL MARKETS

Markets across the world do not usually move in the same direction at the same time. As you construct a strong investment portfolio, you want to increase the probability that the asset classes you own are increasing in value. International markets can be a component of this balance because of their ability to even out US market swings.

The first decade of the 2000s is nicknamed "the lost decade" because the total return of the S&P 500 (an index of the 500 largest companies in the United States) during that time was slightly less than zero. However, international stocks did quite well in this same time period, and people who had certain international stocks in their portfolios saw growth of 6 or 7 percent. It's impossible to predict when these fluctuations will happen, and for that reason, it's prudent to own profitable economic activity all over the world.

US markets break down to large, medium, and small sizes, and similarly, international markets are broken into two categories: developed and emerging (each of which are also further subdivided into large, medium, and small market sizes).

Developed international markets include companies in countries with developed markets and regulations, such as Canada, Germany, Japan, Australia, and France. These markets have perceived stability, and often experience less fluctuation than emerging markets.

Emerging markets include companies in countries with a history of less-reliable markets and economies. The big four emerging markets are Brazil, Russia, India, and China, who are all relatively new to the public stock market. The interaction between governments and companies influences performance in a given market, and emerging markets tend to have interesting relationships between government and business. For example, many companies in China are still state controlled, and a lack of free market participation informs stock prices. Reporting requirements also vary in international markets, which affects their stability.

When emerging markets move, they tend to move big. Emerging economies tend to be driven by commodities and exports, and this affects—and often benefits—their performance. Emerging markets are the most volatile asset class, but because these markets tend to react to different influences and at different times than US markets, they can have a stabilizing effect on a portfolio that increases returns. Emerging markets don't always go against the grain of US markets—the 2008 financial crisis was a notable example of worldwide market influences—but they can provide needed diversity. Mixing different asset classes can counterbalance a portfolio, so that when one asset class goes down, another might be going up.

It's important to evaluate how each investment affects the overall mix of a portfolio and how these markets offset each other. With careful choices, you can dial in the amounts of each market that will maximize growth while keeping risk within tolerances that match your goals.

DIVERSIFYING INHERITANCE

When you inherit a portfolio from a loved one, it's likely that the mix of assets that served them isn't in line with your own goals and needs. Due to the market trends we've discussed, it is common for people of older generations to hold stock portfolios that contain a heavy mix of stocks from large US companies. This can be a good strategy during certain market trends—historically, large US companies do very well—but market conditions shift over time. A balanced portfolio takes into account the individual's needs for return, their tolerance for risk, and the current market conditions. With a step up in cost basis, inheriting a portfolio presents a beautiful opportunity to diversify.

When you create an investment mix that's nicely balanced for your needs, it increases your probability of success in meeting your future financial goals. More important than the value of the investments themselves is whether those investments support the life you want to live. In Bethany's case, her aunt's legacy opened up new possibilities for the dreams Bethany could pursue.

Chapter Seven

ESTATE
PLANNING
AFTER CHAOS

As we sorted and organized my sister's estate, we found keys everywhere. It started with a pile of keys, about fifty of them, thrown on a little table by her front door. I scooped them up and put them in a gallon freezer bag, and as we cleaned out the rest of her house, we found more keys to add. By the end, the bag had about eighty unlabeled keys all jumbled together.

Countless times, when we came across a lock, we had to root through the bag of keys and try a handful at a time. When we found a key that fit, we labeled it and put it on a key ring. Even with this large cache of keys, we still found locks we couldn't open. After an unsuccessful hunt through the key bag, we cut the locks off a shed with bolt cutters. I was surprised by how much frustration and anxiety was caused by this disorganized mess of keys. We spent so much time just trying to unlock things.

After this experience, I collected my own keys on a single ring. There is always enough chaos without having to spend time trying to find the right key for the right lock.

With the role of executor comes pressure and anxiety over settling a loved one's affairs the way they intended. You have to know precisely what your loved one owned and where they wanted those assets to end up. You're constantly looking for the keys to understand how each piece should be managed.

In your own estate, if you can lay out the map of where your assets are and what your intentions are for them, it's a gift for the person who will settle that for you.

THE FIRST SIMPLE STEP

Just as you would gather papers and account statements together to understand your loved one's finances, you can begin your own estate planning simply by compiling all of your information into one place. I recommend a notebook where you can record all of the important information someone may need to understand your accounts and finances. The notebook should contain:

- Your will
- Your power of attorney
- Your Social Security number
- Copies of your driver's license and insurance cards
- Labeled keys
- List of bills and account numbers
- Most recent investment statements
- Most recent year's tax return
- Email accounts and passwords
- Contact information for your lawyer, CPA, and financial advisor
- Contact information for close friends and family
- Titles to your house, car, and other assets, along with service records

Keep this notebook in a secure place where a trusted loved one can access it. This could be a safe for which a friend or family member has the code. This small step of organization will ensure that your loved one has everything they need to resolve your estate, and it will save the time and chaos of finding each of these pieces to begin.

CHECK YOUR BENEFICIARY DESIGNATIONS

As you now know from the previous chapters, each of your

retirement accounts has a beneficiary designation. These can't be changed after your death, and even if your will states that your retirement accounts should go to certain people, those wishes won't be honored if your beneficiary designations don't match your intentions.

Updating your beneficiary information is easy, and I recommend you review your designations every year. Should you decide to change them, it's a simple matter of requesting a change form from the institution, noting the correct beneficiaries, signing the form, and sending it back to the institution to file. Keeping these up to date ensures that your wishes will be carried out.

FORESIGHT IN FINANCES

Every estate plan begins with an initial conversation about unforeseen circumstances. As of this writing, my daughter is twelve years old. If I were to die or become incapacitated, I would need someone to take care of my daughter. It's important for the person who would take over her care to have access to everything they need to pay the bills and cover her care. It's a big decision to choose a guardian for your child, and I've encountered clients who have considered the question but never acted because they couldn't agree on who the guardian should be.

Unforeseen tragedies happen, and in the midst of that

chaos, clear directives are a gift. Collaborating with a financial advisor can help you consider the possible scenarios that could affect your legacy.

For example, I advised a couple who wanted to leave their assets to their two daughters. Both daughters were married, and one of the daughters had kids. This couple needed to consider how the marriages would affect the inheritance: if something were to happen to one of the daughters, their son-in-law would receive the assets intended for the daughter. If they instead wished for that money to be passed to their grandchildren or their other daughter, it would be important to document those wishes ahead of time.

In a scenario like this one, structures can be put in place to clarify the pathway of inheritance. A trust is a great way to set up this structure.

ESTABLISHING A TRUST

There are several different kinds of trusts that can be put in place to dictate how your assets are inherited. In the simplest terms, a trust is an agreement that allows a person to create an account to hold funds, with clear rules for how it is to be distributed to another person or organization. Once a trust is established, it can be managed like any other investment or bank account.

Creating a trust allows you to dictate exactly what rules must be followed as the funds are distributed. When it comes to settling an estate, an IRA is passed directly to the named beneficiary. Bank accounts are transferred to the heirs named in the will. Trusts, however, bypass the will and are not subject to probate. They are a tool to pass wealth directly to another person, charity, or institution, along the guidelines that you draft in the trust agreement.

The rules for distribution on a trust can be as restrictive or free as the owner desires. A trust set up for a younger person, for example, may have rules in place to only distribute a percentage of the trust's value per year, so that those investments can continue to grow and provide wealth over the person's life.

Additionally, the way the trust is structured impacts the way taxes are handled on the funds. Certain trusts are required to be reported on the grantor's tax return, while other types of trusts are assigned their own tax identification number and reported separately. It's important to consider how the tax structure would affect both the grantor and the recipient as you decide what kind of trust to establish.

While an estate planning attorney is needed to draw up a trust, a financial advisor can help set the framework for estate planning conversations. I begin by asking questions to understand how my clients want to pass on their legacy. What do you ultimately want to happen with your assets? Who would you like to inherit your money? How much control do you want? When do you want your loved ones to be able to access these assets? Do you want ongoing access to the trust fund you've created before you die?

Each of these questions helps us look at the big picture together and begin to create a strategy for inheritance. A trust cannot only dictate the rules for how wealth should be passed on, but it can also be of great benefit to an executor: when assets are distributed through a trust, they bypass probate (the proving of the will) and can be transferred directly to the heirs.

There are several different types of trusts that provide the framework for rules of inheritance, and we'll take a brief look at each kind.

Irrevocable Trust

A very common type of trust is an irrevocable trust, which allows you to put money into an account as a gift. Once you contribute money to this type of account, you can no longer access it. Because contributions are considered a "completed gift" for tax purposes, this kind of trust can be a helpful tax tool.

Revocable Trust

With this type of trust, you can set up an account to function similarly to an investment account, in that the rules allow you to maintain complete and full access to the money. Under this structure, you can still use the money during your lifetime, but you can make it easy for your executor because the trust dictates how your wealth is to be transferred automatically to your heirs.

Testamentary Trust

A testamentary trust becomes active upon the death of the account owner. This type of trust can be set up so that, upon death, all liquid assets get retitled in the name of the trust, and then distributed according to the rules of the trust. This is the kind of trust I have set up for my daughter. It won't contain any funds until I die, at which point it will be automatically funded and then distributed to my daughter. Additionally, the rules of the trust are set up so that she won't have immediate access; the funds will be distributed at different stages and ages of her life.

Specialty Trust

Specialty trusts are used in the case of an heir with a disability. If an heir is taking government benefits, but they begin receiving distributions from an inheritance, the distributions could raise their income and cause them to become ineligible for their benefits. A specialty trust can be used to structure the distributions to avoid ineligibility.

Donor-Advised Fund

A cousin of trusts, a donor-advised fund is often used to distribute assets to charity. For tax purposes, contributions to this type of fund are considered completed gifts—meaning that the money you put into this type of fund can be claimed as a donation on your taxes, and can't be transferred back to your personal ownership. Once you've put money into a donor-advised fund, you can manage how it grows through investments, and make distributions to eligible registered charities at any pace you designate. Donor-advised funds are sometimes used as family team-building tools, managed by family members who come together to make decisions about how to distribute the fund.

THE BENEFITS OF A TRUST

While creating a trust requires careful planning, paperwork, and collaboration with an estate attorney, it carries immense benefits for your survivors, who will have clear directions for how your legacy will be inherited.

In our example of the two married daughters above, a trust would ensure that the clients' assets would eventually be inherited by their grandchildren if anything were to happen to their daughters. Trusts can also protect funds from being misused. In the trust I have set up for my young daughter, the distributions are spread out across her life to minimize the risk of spending the money too early.

When you draft a trust with an attorney, you'll choose a trustee. The role of the trustee is to oversee the assets in the trust and make sure they're invested and distributed properly. The trustee's directions are written in the trust; they are responsible for executing the mandate.

When I worked in a trust department, one of our clients was an older woman whose husband had died. He had written a trust that dictated she get a certain amount of money each year, and she did not feel it was sufficient money. She pleaded with us that her husband intended to have a higher standard of living, and that may have been true. However, we had to abide by the trust documents. The bank was acting as trustee for the account, and she was out of luck. While unfortunate stories like this do happen, more often a trust gives peace of mind and security to survivors that they can be assured their loved one's assets are being distributed according to their wishes.

SECURING DECISION-MAKING

The final pieces to consider in your estate planning are setting up power of attorney and medical directives. These additional pieces can be drafted by an attorney, and they are crucial documents to guide your loved ones in case of your incapacity. As we defined in chapter 1, a power of attorney gives decision-making authority to someone to handle your financial accounts. It's also possible to set up a medical power of attorney or advanced medical directive to give a loved one the authority to make medical decisions for you.

By organizing and planning your own affairs, you can take many potential emergencies off the plate of your survivors. In part, estate planning is about creating structures to ensure that your wishes for your legacy are carried out. More than that, this process is about planning for the futures you don't intend. What if the outcome you depend on isn't what actually ends up happening for you? Setting up structures to deal with this uncertainty will give peace of mind not only for yourself but for your survivors.

CONCLUSION

I recently attended the funeral of a client. It was a sweet celebration of her life, and I was struck by how fondly she was remembered by her family. In paying my respects, I thought once more of how important it is to leave a positive legacy behind. My desire to help others leave a clear and impactful legacy is what drove the creation of this book.

There are so many pieces of our lives that are left behind when we die. In addition to the organizational and logistical pressures of settling an estate, the death of a loved one carries financial and emotional weight. So often these pieces are left scattered.

No one considers the work that goes into cleaning out a house after they die. No one thinks of the time it takes to pack up a truck's worth of items to take to Goodwill, or find lost papers and throw away redundant ones, or make multiple trips to the DMV or the bank or the investment institution. When you're suddenly given this job, it can be tremendously overwhelming, but the anxiety and pressure can be relieved by taking one step at a time.

This process is managed through small victories. You'll start with a big jumble of papers, and your first step will be to clean them up and organize them. With that small step done, the next achievable step will be clear. Slowly, bit by bit, you will develop a plan of action.

Rely on the professionals you enlist to help you. You don't need to know everything to take the next small step toward resolving an estate. Professionals can offer shortcuts, shoulders to lean on, and safeguards to avoid mistakes.

Once the estate begins to settle, and it's time to turn your attention to your own inheritance, it can be difficult at first to allow yourself to envision your future goals. You can look to your existing relationships for support, begin to build new ones, and slowly start to identify the accounts and investments that will support your goals.

One step at a time, you can put the puzzle of your loved one's estate back together and begin to develop the picture of your own financial future.

Since going through this process with the deaths of my husband and my sister, I have become even more organized about my own estate. I've begun putting all my financial details into a concise notebook. I've communicated to loved ones what my financial situation looks like and what my wishes are. I have clear plans for who would care for my daughter if something were to happen to me.

These systems aren't perfect yet, but I'm continuing to learn and refine them. When it is time to celebrate my life, I know my loved ones will have a clear plan ahead of them for resolving my estate, so they can focus on supporting each other. That is the legacy I want to leave behind. Whether you're organizing your loved one's estate or your own, you're currently developing the awareness, knowledge, and tools to leave a bright legacy of your own.

ABOUT THE AUTHOR

JENNIFER LUZZATTO is a Chartered Financial Analyst®, a Certified Financial Planner®, and a NAPFA-registered financial advisor. She began her career in financial services thirty years ago as a fixed-income trader in a regional brokerage firm and went on to manage personal trust accounts, institutional portfolios, and a municipal bond mutual fund at a commercial bank. In 1999, she founded Summit Financial Partners, transitioning from banking to financial planning and investment advisory services. Jennifer holds a BA in psychology and an MBA from the University of Richmond. She lives in Richmond, Virginia, with her daughter and their dog.